Helping Children See Jesus

ISBN: 978-1-933206-64-6

SERVANTS OF GOD
The Epistles Set 1
2 Corinthians

Author: R. Iona Lyster
Illustrator: Frances H. Hertzler
Computer Graphic Artist: Ed Olson
Typesetting and Layout: Patricia Pope

© 2018 Bible Visuals International
PO Box 153, Akron, PA 17501-0153
Phone: (717) 859-1131
www.biblevisuals.org

All rights reserved. No part of this publication may be reproduced, stored in a retrieval system or transmitted in any form by any means, electronic, mechanical, photocopy, recording or otherwise, without the prior permission of the publisher, except as provided by USA copyright law

RELATED ITEMS

To access related items (such as activities, memory verse posters and translated texts) please visit our web store at shop.biblevisuals.org and enter 1025 in the search box on the page.

FREE TEXT DOWNLOAD

To access a FREE printable copy of the teaching text (PDF format) in English or other available languages, enter S1025DL in the search box. Add the item to your cart, and use coupon code XTACSV17 at checkout. Once your order is processed you will receive an email with a link to the free download.

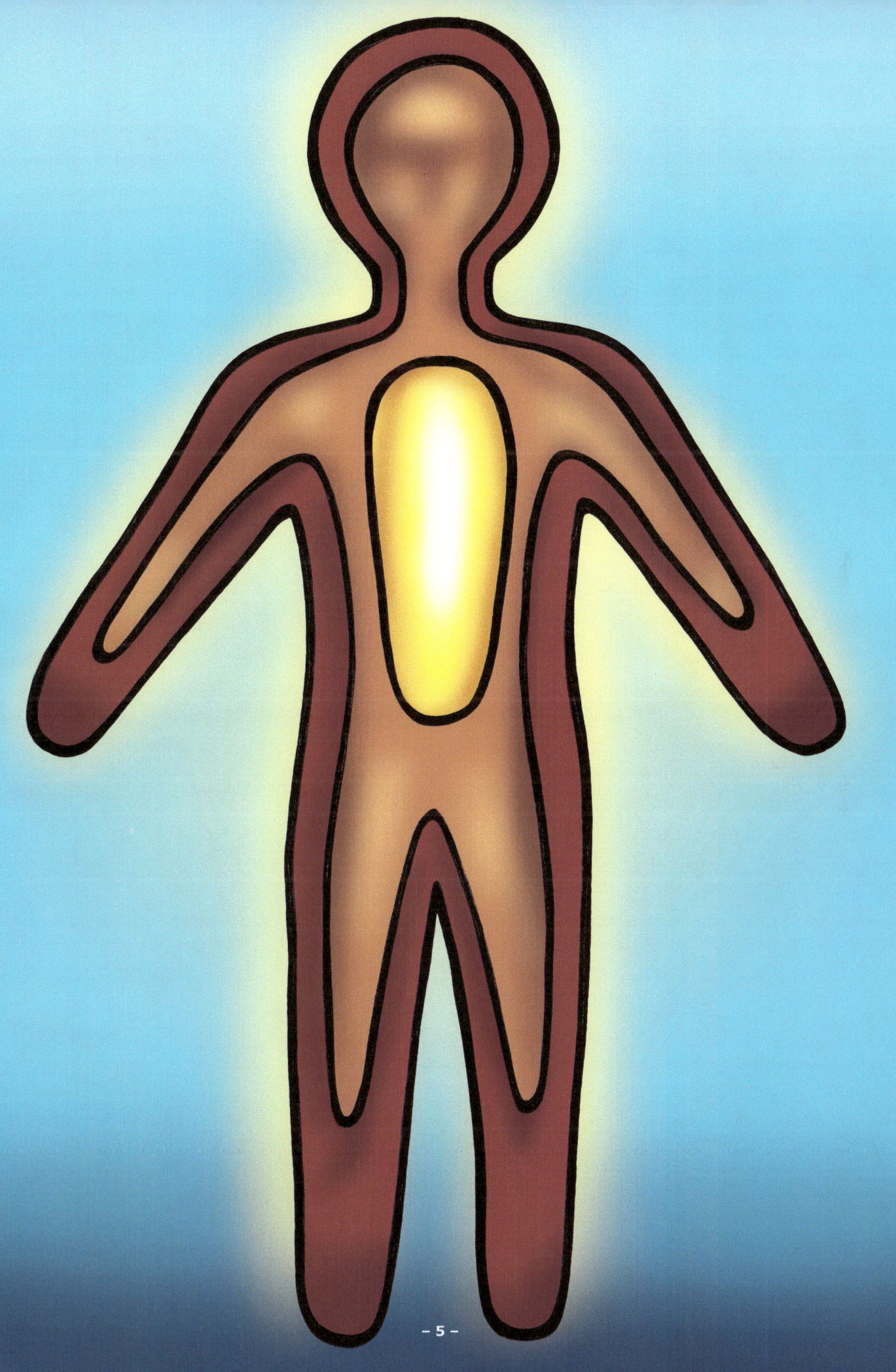

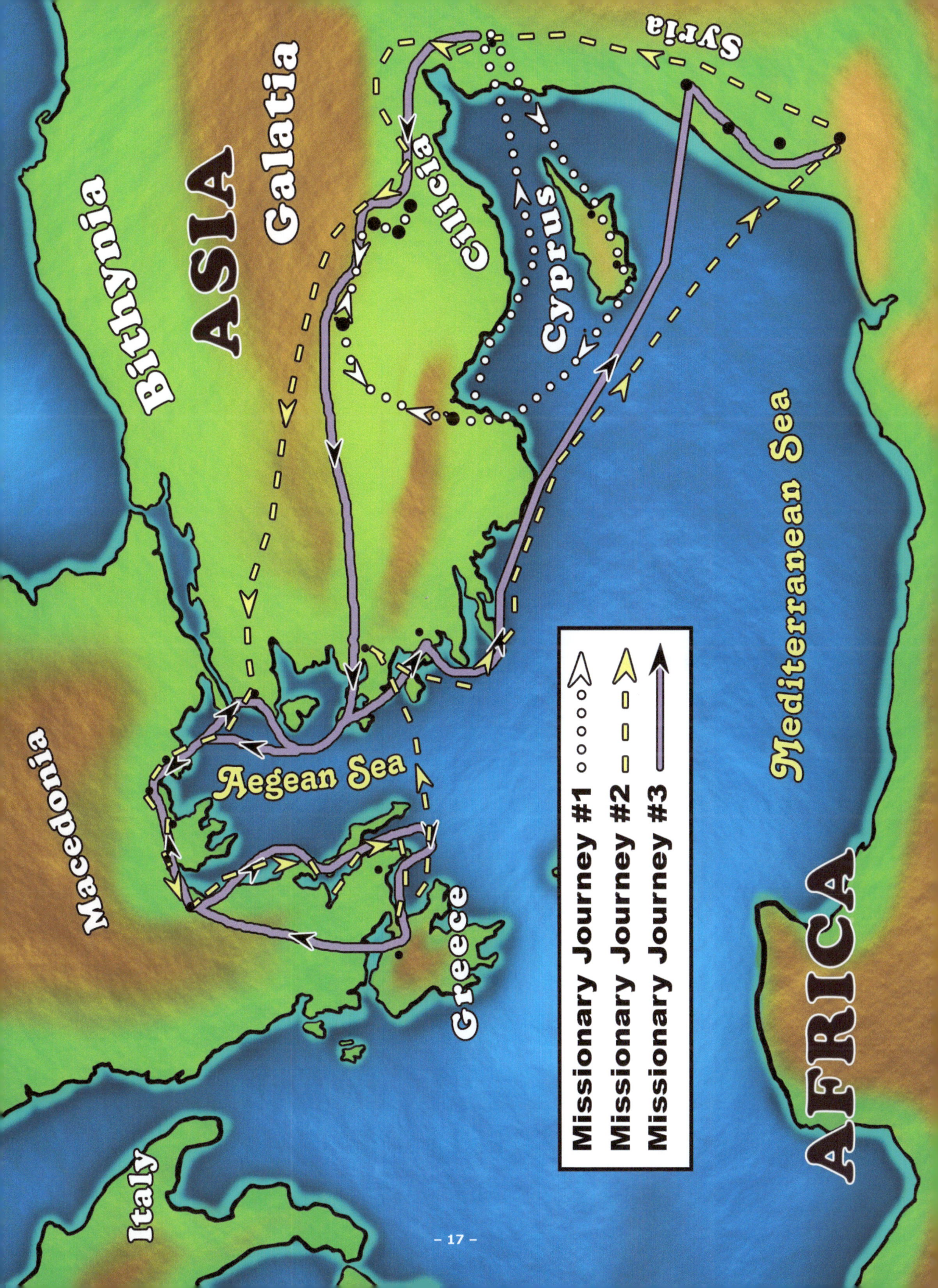

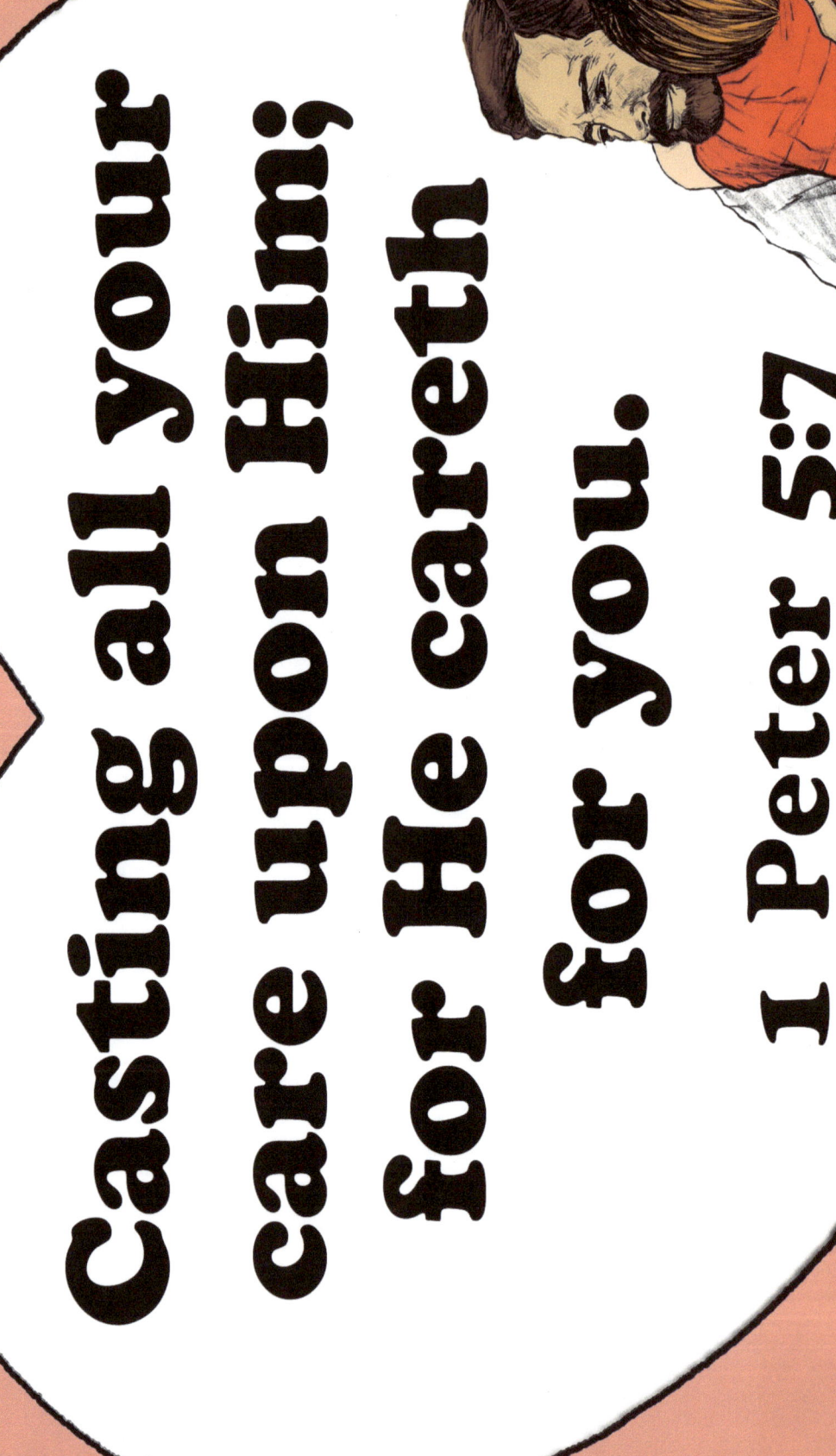

Casting all your care upon Him; for He careth for you.

1 Peter 5:7

Thanks be unto God for His unspeakable gift.
2 Corinthians 9:15

Lesson 1
GOD TAKES CARE OF HIS SERVANTS

Scripture to be studied: 2 Corinthians 1-4, 10-12

The *aim* of the lesson: No matter what difficulty a believer has when he/she is serving God, God will care for him/her and supply everything he/she needs.

What your students should *know*: Because God cares and comforts believers, they should comfort others.

What your students should *feel*: A desire to help someone in need.

What your students should *do*: Ask the Lord to make them conscious of the needs of others so they can share Gods comfort with them.

Lesson outline (for the teachers and students' notebooks):

1. Paul escapes from those who tried to kill him.
2. Paul survives a shipwreck.
3. Paul is stoned, but God gives Him a glimpse into Heaven.
4. God allows Paul's problem to remain so He can show him His strength.

The verse to be memorized:

Casting all your care upon Him, for He careth for you. (l Peter 5:7)

NOTE TO THE TEACHER

In one way or another all who belong to Christ are servants of God. Some may give more time to serving Him. But all of us–old and young–are God's servants. Therefore the lessons of this series should be very helpful to each child of God.

THE LESSON

Do you remember a time when you were young that you fell and hurt yourself? What did you do? You ran home to Mother, crying. And what did she do? She comforted you. She may have held you, or perhaps she washed the hurt with cool water. Soon you felt better. How is it that mothers know how to comfort their children? It was because when they were little, their own mothers comforted them.

In Paul's second letter to the Corinthians he tells of the many times that he, God's servant, needed comfort. He explains that because God comforted him, he can comfort others who have hard times in their lives. Later those whom he has comforted will be able to comfort others, he says. (See 2 Corinthians 1:3-6.)

The Apostle Paul was possibly the greatest of all missionaries. He took the Gospel to hundreds and thousands who had never heard it. He gladly served God with all his heart. Why should such a missionary need to be comforted? What kind of hurts did he have? He tells us the answers to these questions in 2 Corinthians. This is what he says. (*Teacher:* Depending on the ability of your pupils, you may wish to read 2 Corinthians 11:23-28.):

I have been whipped many times.

I have often been in jail.

Many times I was in danger of death.

Five times I had 39 lashes across my back.

I was beaten three times.

Once I was stoned.

I was shipwrecked three times.

I was in the water a day and a night.

I have been in danger in water, in danger of robbers, in danger of people in my own country, in danger of those of other countries, in danger in the city, in danger in the wilds, in danger on the sea.

I have been tired and full of pain.

I have been hungry and thirsty.

I have gone without food.

I have been cold and naked.

I have had to take care of all the churches which were just getting started.

I had to escape one city by being let down over the wall in a basket.

Poor Paul! How he did need comfort!

1. PAUL ESCAPES FROM THOSE WHO TRIED TO KILL HIM

If Paul could be here today, we might question him about his experiences. For example, maybe we would ask, "Why did you have to escape from one city in a basket?"

Paul would doubtless answer, "That was one of my first experiences after I was saved. (See Acts 9:23-25.) I had returned to the city of Damascus and preached the Gospel of Jesus Christ to the Jews. They knew that once I, a Jew, had hated Christians and had come to their city to kill them or put them in prison. Now because I had turned to Christ, the Jews hated me and wanted to kill me just as I myself had previously wanted to kill Christians. Day and night they watched the city gates so I could not escape.

Show Illustration #1

"But one night when it was completely dark, I got into a basket. Quietly and oh-so-carefully, friends let me down over the city wall. Outside the wall, I tiptoed from one shadow to another. When I was certain no one had heard me, I ran fast and escaped. I was safe! I was a servant of God. And God takes care of his own."

Why did Paul have to escape from Damascus? He had preached the Gospel. That was all. But because those who heard hated the Lord Jesus Christ about whom Paul preached, they planned to kill him.

2. PAUL SURVIVES A SHIPWRECK

If Paul were here today we would certainly say, "Tell us about one of the times you were shipwrecked, Paul."

"I'll tell you about my last shipwreck. I was a prisoner on a ship bound for Rome. (See Acts 27:1–28:15.) Do you know why I was a prisoner? I had been preaching the Gospel of Christ. (See Acts 25:21–26:22.) As usual, some people didn't want to hear the Good News. Because they hated my message, they hated me. So I was being sent to Rome for trial.

"Our ship was not comfortable and we knew the sea voyage would be a long one. (*Teacher:* Luke joined Paul for the journey. Luke is the one who wrote the book of Acts, you will recall. So when you see the words *we* and *us* beginning in Acts 27:2, you know that Luke and Paul were together.) We left in late summer, made many stops and changed ships along the way. We hoped to be able to spend the winter in a good harbor. But before we could get there, a strong wind caught us. Although the men in charge of the ship did all they could to lighten the load, they finally had to let the ship run with the wind.

"An angel from God had promised me that no lives would be lost; so I explained this to the sailors. I told them, too, that we would be cast up on some island.

"The wind and storm continued for 14 days and nights.

Show Illustration #2

"Finally we landed in a narrow channel, and the violent waves broke up the ship. The sailors wanted to kill us prisoners. But the man in charge would not permit it. So those who could, swam to shore. The rest clung to boards and broken pieces of the ship, and we all got to the beach safely. Not one was lost, just as the angel of God had promised!

"When we got on land the local men built a fire to warm us. We were wet from the sea, wet from the rain, and the weather was cold. I helped to gather sticks for the fire. As I did, a snake fastened on my hand to bite me. When the island people saw it, they thought I must be a murderer and was therefore being punished. But I shook the snake off into the fire and felt nothing. The islanders thought I should have become swollen or fallen down dead. But when nothing happened to me, they changed their minds and thought I must be a god.

"During the three months we were there, God did many miracles through us, His servants. Nothing compares with the joy of belonging to Him. Even in a shipwreck He cares for His own and uses us for Himself."

3. PAUL IS STONED BUT GOD GIVES HIM A GLIMPSE INTO HEAVEN

"Now, Paul, tell us about the time you were stoned."

"That happened when Barnabas and I were serving the Lord in the city of Lystra. (See Acts 14:8-20.) Once when I was preaching I could tell by looking at a crippled man who was in the crowd that he believed the message. So right in the middle of my sermon I commanded him, saying, 'Stand up on your feet.' That moment, though the man had never taken a step in his whole life, he jumped up and walked.

"When the people saw this they decided that Barnabas and I were gods and they prepared to worship us. Immediately we told them that we were only servants of the Most High God and of His Son, the Saviour, Jesus Christ.

"Shortly after that some Jews (from Antioch and Iconium– 100 miles away) came to Lystra and stirred up the people against us. Then that same crowd, which had wanted to worship us, hurled stones at me.

Show Illustration #3

"The pain was unbearable and I collapsed. What happened after that was not clear to me. But I now know they dragged me out of the city and left me for dead. I think it was at that time that a wonderful thing happened to me. I was given a glimpse of Heaven! The things I saw and heard were too wonderful for me to describe. (See 2 Corinthians 12:2-4.)

"Suddenly it was all over. When I opened my eyes, I was glad to see that my friends had found me. All of us realized that God had more work for me to do here on earth. The next day, amazingly, I was better and we were able to leave to preach in Derbe. The stoning–as awful as it was–was a wonderful experience. For if I had not been stoned, I might never have had that glimpse of Heaven."

4. GOD ALLOWS PAUL'S PROBLEM TO REMAIN SO HE CAN SHOW PAUL HIS STRENGTH

"I must tell you this, however. There are times when God chooses not to rescue us from our problems. To keep me from being too proud after I had the glimpse of Heaven, God gave me a problem–I called it my 'thorn in the flesh.' It was a dreadful thing for me. Three times I begged the Lord to remove it. (See 2 Corinthians 12:1-10.)

Show Illustration #4

"But instead of removing the problem–my 'thorn'–God answered, 'My loving favor is all you need. My strength is perfect in weak people.' I'm content to have my problem, so that I may have Christ's power."

Paul learned tremendous truths when he was here on earth long ago. He has shared those truths with us. Because God is a kind, loving heavenly Father, He takes care of us in all our troubles. Sometimes He removes the trouble. Other times He makes it possible for us to keep right on going, even with the troublesome thing. And because of His comfort to us, His children, we can–and should–comfort others who have similar problems.

Do you know someone whom you can help this week? Perhaps you will want to tell them about Paul's problems. Or maybe you will want to quote our memory verse. Will you ask God to make you alert to the needs of others so you can give His comfort to someone who needs it?

Lesson 2
THE DEATH OF GOD'S SERVANTS

NOTE TO THE TEACHER

Are you afraid to die? Many people are. But Christians need not fear death. Because the Lord Jesus Christ rose from the dead, those who believe in Him will also rise from the dead. So you never need to be afraid to die. (See Hebrews 2:14-15.)

Before you begin your study, write down what you believe happens after a person dies. Then, asking the Lord's help, read the lesson carefully. Look up all the additional Scriptures that are mentioned. Compare God's Word with what you thought. Are there differences? Do you understand what God has said? Do you still dread to die?

Your students, no matter what age, need this lesson. They must be prepared to die. People die at all ages, young as well as old. You could start the lesson by asking, "Are you afraid to die?" "Why?" "What do you think will happen to you after you die?" "Do you know what God says about this?" They do not have to answer the questions aloud. But they ought to think about them and then study to find out what God says.

At the end of the lesson if you feel that your students are still afraid to die, you should try to determine the reason for their fear. It may be that some sin is disturbing them. They ought to confess this to God and ask for His peace and for an understanding of what lies beyond death for the Christian.

Scripture to be studied: 2 Corinthians 4:17-5:10; Luke 16:19-31; 23:39-45; 1 Thessalonians 4:13-17; Revelation 20:11-15

The *aim* of the lesson: The servant of God may face death, but he need not fear it if he is prepared to stand before the Lord Jesus Christ.

What your students should *know*: The Lord wants every believer to serve Him with a pure heart.

What your students should *feel*: A desire to be sincere, earnest servants of the Lord.

What your students should *do*: Ask the Lord what He wants them to do this week and then seek to do what He says.

Lesson outline (for the teacher's and students' notebooks):
1. The body dies but the soul and spirit live forever.
2. After death, those who belong to God go to a place of blessing; unbelievers are separated from God forever.
3. The thief who trusted in Jesus went to be with Jesus when he died.
4. The works of believers will be tested at the Judgment Seat of Christ.

The verse to be memorized:

Casting all your care upon Him; for He careth for you. (1 Peter 5:7)

THE LESSON

In his second letter to the Corinthians the Apostle Paul said that we who are servants of God are to comfort those who are in trouble. Who will tell us how you obeyed that instruction during the past week? (Let your pupils tell their experiences of comforting others.)

In this same important letter Paul teaches about the death of God's servants. What happens after death? Suppose you were to die today. Where would your body go? Where would you go? The Corinthians needed to know the answers to these questions. And so do we. Our Bible has the answers.

1. THE BODY DIES BUT THE SOUL AND SPIRIT LIVE FOREVER

When you and I look at each other, we don't see the entire person. We simply see the outside of the person–and what he or she does. We don't see what that person is like in his heart. Our bodies, the Bible tells us, are like houses. (See 2 Corinthians 5:1-4.) Perhaps you have noticed two houses alongside each other. One is dark and silent because it is empty. You say, "Things are dead in that house." But the next house is lighted, and you hear singing and talking and laughing. And you say, "That house is alive." It is not the house that is dead or alive. It's what is in it, or what is not inside it, that makes it alive or dead.

Show Illustration #5

So it is with you. As long as you are in your "body-house," you are alive. But when you die, your "body-house"–the part of you which others can see–will be silent and empty. Your body will have to be buried for it will decay quickly. Although the "body-house" you live in may die, your spirit and soul will not die but will live forever. (To see that you have a spirit, soul and body, read 1 Thessalonians 5:23 and Hebrews 4:12.) Your soul is the part of you which makes you conscious of God. It is the part of you that causes you to want to talk to God. Your spirit is the part of you which *knows*. (See 1 Corinthians 2:11.) Where you will live after you die is decided by you before you die. If you belong to God (because you have trusted in His Son), your spirit and soul will go to live with Christ forever. If you have refused to trust in Him, you must live apart from Him forever.

The bodies of believers and unbelievers remain in their graves until their resurrection day. The bodies of Christian believers will be raised from the dead when the Lord Jesus comes in the air to take His own to be with Him. In some miraculous way each believer's body (which has returned to dust) will be raised and joined with its spirit and soul and caught up to be with the Lord Jesus forever. (See 1 Corinthians 15:51-53; 1 Thessalonians 4:13-18.) The bodies of unbelievers will be raised 1,000 years later. (See Revelation 20:5.)

2. AFTER DEATH, THOSE WHO BELONG TO GOD GO TO A PLACE OF BLESSING; UNBELIEVERS ARE SEPARATED FROM GOD FOREVER

Although bodies are in graves after death, the part of the person known as the spirit and soul is very much alive. The

Apostle Paul said that when we no longer live in these bodies, we are with Christ. (See 2 Corinthians 5:6, 8.) Being with Christ, he said, is "far better." (See Philippians 1:23.)

How did Paul know that it was far better to be with Christ? He was once caught up into the third heaven. What he saw was so beautiful and so wonderful that he could not even describe it. (See 2 Corinthians 12:2-4.) He was perfectly intelligent and perfectly happy in Heaven, even though he did not have his body with him.

The Lord Jesus once told about two men—a rich man and a poor beggar named Lazarus. The rich man, He said, had fine clothing and the best of food. Lazarus begged for crumbs at the rich man's gate. Lazarus had bad sores which the dogs licked.

In time, both men died. Lazarus the beggar, because he had trusted in God, was carried by the angels to a place of blessing. There he was with Abraham, the "father" of those who believe God. Lazarus' body had been buried in the earth, but his soul and spirit were in the place of blessing.

Show Illustration #6

The rich man had not believed God. So when he died he went to a place of suffering. He was far away from Abraham and the beggar, far away from help. His body had probably been buried in a place of honor. But his spirit and soul continued on, far from God and all that was good. He cried out, "Father Abraham, have pity on me. Send Lazarus to me. Let him put the tip of his finger in water and cool my tongue. I am tormented in this flame."

Abraham answered, "There is a great space between us. Even if anyone here wanted to come to you, they couldn't do so. And no one from where you are can come here."

The rich man answered, "Then please send Lazarus to my family. I have five brothers. Let him warn them so they won't come to this place . . . . If someone goes to them from the dead, and tells them how awful it is here, they will be sorry for their sins and turn to God."

"No," Abraham answered. "If they won't listen to the Word of God given by Moses and the prophets, they won't listen even if someone could go to them from the dead."

Before he died, the rich man had not turned to God. After his death, he could do nothing about changing the place where he went. There he would be tormented forever and ever.

3. THE THIEF WHO TRUSTED IN JESUS WENT TO BE WITH JESUS WHEN HE DIED

Show Illustration #7

On the day that the Lord Jesus was nailed to a cross, two wicked men were crucified also.

One of them cried to Jesus, "If you are the One sent from God, save Yourself and us."

The other rebuked him, saying, "Aren't you afraid of God? We're dying because we deserve to die. But this Man hasn't done anything wrong." Then, turning to the Lord Jesus, he said, "Jesus, Lord, remember me when You come into Your kingdom."

Because the Lord Jesus knew what was in the heart of each man, he knew that the second man had repented and trusted in Him. So He said to him, "Today you will be with Me in a place of blessing." (See Luke 23:39-45.) His "body-house" would be placed in the grave. But his spirit and soul would be with Jesus immediately.

If the Lord Jesus does not come for believers during our lifetime, we shall die. Our bodies will be put into graves. But our spirits and souls will go to be with Him immediately. What could be more wonderful than being with Christ? Nothing! So we don't need to be afraid to die.

4. THE WORKS OF BELIEVERS WILL BE TESTED AT THE JUDGMENT SEAT OF CHRIST

Later, when all believers have been caught up together to meet the Lord in the air, we shall stand before the Judgment Seat of Christ. (Read 2 Corinthians 5:10 to your class, please.) We will not be judged to determine if we will go to Heaven. That was decided when we received the Lord Jesus Christ as Saviour here on earth.

Show Illustration #8

But at the Judgment Seat of Christ, everything we have done since we became Christians will be tested. If the things we did on earth have been done to please the Lord, they will stand the test of fire as do gold, silver and precious stones. If we have done things to get honor for ourselves, they will go up in smoke, as do wood and hay and dry grass. (See 1 Corinthians 3:12-15.)

When Paul wrote these words, he was probably thinking of something that had happened in the city of Ephesus. There was in Ephesus a magnificent temple of Diana. Because it was built on marshy ground, a great foundation of rock had to be laid. And that foundation took years to build. The building was built almost entirely of gold, silver and costly stones. But the roof and the rooms that were built onto the main part of the building were made of wood, hay and dry grass. These rooms were used by the priests and priestesses of Diana. One night (the night of the birth of the man who was to become known as Alexander the Great), an Ephesian man (Erostratus) set fire to the temple of Diana. In the morning the gold, silver and costly stones were unharmed. But the wood, hay and dry grass were gone–eaten by the flames.

At the Judgment Seat of Christ, fire will test every person's work. It's not how much we have done that will be tested. But the kind of work we have done will have to stand the fire test. Check up on yourself. (See 1 Corinthians 11:31-32.) Are you truly serving God with a pure heart? Our memory verse tells us that God cares for us. Because He does, He wants us to have the best when life is over. He warns us: "Behold, I come quickly; and My reward is with Me, to give each one according as his work shall be" (Revelation 22:12).

Will you ask the Lord, right now, to make you a sincere, earnest servant always? Ask Him what you can do for Him this week. Do this every week, every day. Then if you do what He tells you to do, you can trust Him for rewards when you stand at His Judgment Seat.

Lesson 3
THE MESSAGE OF GOD'S SERVANTS (RECONCILIATION)

NOTE TO THE TEACHER

In this series we have studied that (1) God cares for His servants in their tests and trials; and (2) although His servants do not need to be afraid of death, each one must be prepared to stand before the Judgment Seat of Christ. Now, in this lesson, we learn about reconciliation, the message which servants of God must share with others.

You will want to study the verses that have to do with reconciliation: Romans 5:10; 2 Corinthians 5:18-20; Ephesians 2:16; Colossians 1:20-22. Reconcile means to restore to favor because of a thorough change. All people everywhere have turned away from God. Turning from God is sin. Sin causes a barrier between God and man. But because the Lord Jesus gave His blood, God is able to show mercy to those who deserve judgment, changing them completely and restoring them to His favor. God alone makes reconciliation possible. Man has no part in it. But man does have a part in making known the message of reconciliation. It is our happy privilege–and responsibility–to persuade others to receive the reconciliation which the Lord Jesus has accomplished on the cross. We are His ambassadors–his specially chosen messengers. Think of that!

Scripture to be studied: 2 Corinthians 5:10-21; 4:1-3, 5-7; 6:1-18; 11:1-15

The *aim* of the lesson: To help the students to understand the message of reconciliation–and to prepare them so they will share the message with others.

> **What your students should *know*:** Believers in addition to witnessing for Christ should live consistent Christian lives.
>
> **What your students should *feel*:** A desire to share the Gospel with someone.
>
> **What your students should *do*:** Think of some friend who does not know the Lord Jesus. Ask God to help them introduce him/her to the Saviour.

Lesson outline (for the teacher's and students' notebooks):

1. Sinners come short of the glory of God.
2. Those who trust in Christ are reconciled (brought into loving favor with God.)
3. Those who are reconciled are thoroughly changed.
4. Believers should be prepared to tell the Lord with whom they have shared the gospel.

The verse to be memorized:

Casting all your care upon Him; for He careth for you. (1 Peter 5:7)

THE LESSON

Unless the Lord Jesus comes and catches us believers up to be with Him, we will all die. Those of us who are Christians do not need to be afraid of death. The moment we die we will be with the Lord. Only our bodies will be in graves. But the day that Jesus comes for His own, the bodies of dead believers will be raised. Then they, together with living believers, will be caught up to meet the Lord in the air. (See 1 Thessalonians 4:16-18) After that, all Christians will have their works tested as they stand before the Judgment Seat of Christ. We don't have to be afraid to die. But what about standing before the Judgment Seat of Christ? What works will be tested? Will those works be good or worthless? Listen closely!

Just after Paul tells the Corinthians (and us) that we must all appear before the Judgment Seat of Christ, he says, "We are ambassadors for Christ" (2 Corinthians 5:20). This means that God has appointed every believer to be a personal representative of the Lord Jesus. We are to speak His message for Him. This is not something we may do if we choose. It is something we must do. God has made a way for others to come to Him. And He has given us who believe in Him the work of telling others how they can come to Him. (See 2 Corinthians 5:18-19.) Because we are His disciples, we are commanded to speak His message (Matthew 28:18-20; Mark 16:15).

What is His message? It is this: "God is in Christ reconciling the world to Himself," and "You must be reconciled to God." (See 2 Corinthians 5:19-20.) To understand what these statements mean, we must understand the meaning of the word *reconcile*.

1. SINNERS COME SHORT OF THE GLORY OF GOD

God is absolutely perfect in every way. His Son, the Lord Jesus Christ, is absolutely perfect. He never did a wrong thing. He never said a wrong thing. He never thought one wrong thing. He is perfect. But no one else is perfect. We all have done wrong things. We all have said wrong things. We all have thought wrong things. (*Teacher:* Tell something wrong that you did before you were saved, preferably when you were a child, to show that you sinned even when you were young. Then ask your pupils if they have ever done anything wrong. Let them tell about it briefly.) Why do we all do wrong? Because we all are sinners. We all were born sinners. (See Psalm 51:5; 58:3.) So we all come short of God's glory. (See Romans 3:23.)

When we go to market to buy a pound of rice, a pound weight is put on one side of the scale. (*Teacher:* Use the weight of your country. If it's kilo, use that please. Perhaps corn or cotton or peanuts or something else is a more typical in your country than rice. Use whatever it is that your people buy.) To get an equal amount of rice, the scale must balance. The position of the scale is completely changed when it is in balance. But the weight never changes. Everything is measured by the standard of that weight.

Show Illustration #9

Because of sin, all people are out of favor with God. We come short of His glory. So God the Father caused God the Son (One who is equal to Himself) to die on the cross. "God was in Christ" is the message that we share with others. And why was God in Christ? To reconcile the world to Himself.

God loved us long before we were born. He wants us to be His own. But our sin has separated us from Him. We could never do one thing to change ourselves from being sinners. So God gave His own perfect Son to take the death punishment we deserve for our sin.

2. THOSE WHO TRUST IN CHRIST ARE RECONCILED WITH GOD

Show Illustration #10

When we believe that the Lord Jesus is the Son of God who gave His blood for us, when we receive Him as our Saviour, we are thoroughly changed–changed from those who hated God or ignored Him, to those who love Him. That change is known as reconciliation. And God does it all! He gave His Son. His Son gave Himself on the cross. When our trust is in Him, God reconciles us–restores us–to His loving favor. This is the message we are to give to others: you must be reconciled to God.

Long before the Lord Jesus lived on earth, something happened that helps us to appreciate the meaning of reconciliation. The people of Israel had a wicked king–King Saul. Saul knew that God had appointed David, a shepherd, to become the king. And that made King Saul furious–so furious, indeed, that he tried to kill David.

Jonathan (one of Saul's sons) and David loved each other dearly–so dearly that they solemnly promised to take care of each other always. Not only did they agree to take care of one another, but they determined to care for each others family. A time came when both King Saul and his son, Jonathan, were killed in battle. Then David became king of Israel, as God had planned.

One day David remembered his promise to Jonathan. So he sent for Saul's servant and asked, "Are there any members of Sauls family still living?"

"Yes," the servant answered. "Jonathan's son, Mephibosheth, (Saul's grandson) who is lame is still alive."

"Where is he?" David asked.

The servant told him and David sent for Saul's grandson.

3. THOSE WHO ARE RECONCILED ARE THOROUGHLY CHANGED

Mephibosheth was frightened when he came to the king. If King David would do what kings usually did, he would kill Mephibosheth because of his being related to the former king. But David said, "Don't be afraid! I've asked you to come so that I may be kind to you. Because of my love for your father (Jonathan) I am going to give you everything that belonged to your grandfather, Saul. And you shall live here at the palace."

Show Illustration #11

From then on Mephibosheth lived with King David as one of his sons. Everything was completely changed for Mephibosheth. Ordinarily kings didn't even want to see a cripple. But because of the king's love for Jonathan, lame Mephibosheth was reconciled to the king. He was brought into loving favor and harmony with King David.

So it is with us. Once we were afraid of God because of our sins. (See Psalm 5:5.) But when we place our trust in His Son, the Lord Jesus Christ, we are thoroughly changed. Instead of being rebels who hate God or those who ignore Him, we love Him. We are reconciled to Him. We are restored to God's loving favor because of the Lord Jesus.

4. BELIEVERS SHOULD BE PREPARED TO TELL THE LORD WITH WHOM THEY HAVE SHARED THE GOSPEL

One of the proofs that we are His is the fact that we want to share the good news with others. We want to tell them, "You, too, may be reconciled to God."

That is what the Apostle Paul did. Bravely he preached, "Now is the right time! Listen! Today is the day to be saved!" (See 2 Corinthians 6:2.) He knew that he was a personal representative of Christ Jesus. He wanted to share the Gospel with others. And God helped him to take the Good News from one land to another. Do you think that Paul will have to be afraid or ashamed when he stands at the Judgment Seat of Christ?

Show Illustration #12

What about you? If the Lord Jesus comes within the next few days, will you be glad to stand before Him? Suppose He should ask, "With whom have you shared My Gospel?" What would your answer be?

Not everyone has the opportunity of telling the Good News to the world as the Apostle Paul did. But every child of God does have the responsibility of telling the Good News to those around him/her. Have you thought of one whom you would like to introduce to the Lord Jesus? (*Teacher:* You may want to ask for the names and list them on the board. Each student should write the name of his/her friend in his/her notebook.) Even before you go to that person, what should you do first–what could you do right now? Yes, you could pray for him/her by name. We will wait a bit while you pray. (You, teacher, will know whether they should pray for their friends silently or aloud.)

Probably the most important part of our witness to others is our prayer for them. You may be the one to introduce people to the Saviour. But who will show them that they are sinners who need the Saviour? The Holy Spirit. And He can prepare their hearts so that when you talk to them, they will listen to you.

Can you think of something else that is an important part of our witness for Christ? Is there something we should do before we share the Gospel message? (Your students should think about this, teacher. If necessary, ask questions that will help them to see the necessity of living a consistent Christian life every day.) How we live is mighty important. Those to whom we want to take the Gospel message must see that it has affected our lives for good. We are interested in them. We are helpful. We are kind. If we aren't, then our speaking of salvation from sin will not mean much.

You have in your notebook the name of one (or more) whom you want to introduce to the Lord Jesus. Under each name, suppose you list the things you could do this week that would show your friend that you're really interested in him/her. The way we show our interest in one person may be quite different from the way we show our interest in another.

As you think about that particular person, what do you suppose might be a good way to introduce him/her to the Lord Jesus? What could you say that would help your friend to know that the Lord Jesus is your most important, most wonderful Friend? How would you help your friend to understand that Christ is the only One who can change us thoroughly and restore us to God's loving favor? Do you want to write in your notebook something that you might like to say to your friend?

Remember, some day you'll stand before the Judgment Seat of Christ. In that day you will be glad that you were His faithful witness.

(*Teacher:* If you have unsaved students, help them to understand that in order to introduce others to the Saviour they must first belong to Him. Give them an opportunity to receive the Lord Jesus. Have special prayer for all your students–and yourself–that each of you may be faithful in living the Christian life and in witnessing through this coming week.)

Lesson 4
GIVING BY GOD'S SERVANTS

NOTE TO THE TEACHER

This is the last lesson on Pauls letters to the Corinthians. In these two letters, Paul emphasizes Christian living and service. The moment a person trusts Jesus as Saviour, the Holy Spirit makes him a part of the church which is called "the body of Christ." The members of the body of Christ meeting regularly in any place, meet as a church group.

These letters emphasize everyday living and individual service for God as part of a church group. Giving to God is a vital part of Christian living. In each believer's church group, he will learn of the needs of others. If each Christian gives whatever God wants him to give, God's work will be cared for both at home and to the ends of the earth.

This time we have a different memory verse from the one in the first three lessons. This will not be difficult for your pupils to learn. Make it clear that the Lord Jesus Christ is God's "unspeakable Gift."

Scripture to be studied: 2 Corinthians 8:9; 1 Corinthians 16

The *aim* of the lesson: Giving is part of our Christian living. We should learn to give gladly to God.

What your students should *know*: It is important to give God ourselves and our possessions.

What your students should *feel*: A desire to be faithful in giving to the Lord.

What your students should *do*: Give themselves to the Lord right now.

Lesson outline (for the teacher's and students' notebooks):

1. God wants His own to give willingly to Him.
2. God wants His own to give liberally.
3. God wants His own to give lovingly.
4. Christians are to give cheerfully to the Lord.

The verse to be memorized:

Thanks be unto God for his unspeakable gift. (2 Corinthians 9:15)

THE LESSON

Those in the church at Corinth were new believers. Like all new believers everywhere, they had much to learn about Christian living. One of the things about which the Apostle Paul wrote them was the matter of giving to God. Giving is as important a service as any other. It is something that every believer can do and should do. You, like the Corinthians, must know what God says about giving.

A famine had come to Jerusalem and all Judea. It affected everyone–Christians and non-Christians. Unbelievers in other lands who heard of the famine sent help to the unbelievers who were suffering. But who would help the believers? It would have to be other believers, of course. So when the Apostle Paul was in Corinth he told the church about those who were suffering in Jerusalem. Immediately the Corinthians promised Paul that they would help. They would contribute money to the fund that he would take to the Jerusalem Christians.

So when Paul went up north to Macedonia, he bragged to them about the promises made by those down south in Achaia. (Corinth is in Achaia.) And the Macedonians determined that they, too, would help. Actually the Macedonians had very little, because the Romans had robbed them. But they were so eager to share that they begged for the favor of giving. So their gift was a real sacrifice. In fact, even before they gave their gift, they did something that pleased God. They gave themselves to Him to serve and obey Him. That is the kind of giving that God delights in–giving one's life to Him and then giving a gift to Him. That gift may be money which can be used in the Lord's work. Or it may be food or clothing or anything that can be shared with the Lord's people. The gift could even be time for the Lord or helpful work for others.

But a year after Paul had left Corinth the Corinthians had not sent their gift. So Paul told them that his bragging about them had caused the Macedonians to give more than they could afford. Now the Corinthians would be embarrassed if they didn't give. Paul urged them to gather what they had purposed to give. He said they should give willingly as the Macedonians had done. (See 2 Corinthians 8:3.) They should give liberally (as much as they could–or more than they could.) ("See that ye abound in this grace also.") They were to give lovingly. ("Prove the sincerity of your love.") And, he said, their gifts were to be given cheerfully. ("God loveth a cheerful giver.") That is exactly how we, too, should give. (*Teacher:* Have your pupils list in their notebooks these four ways to give to God.)

1. GOD WANTS HIS OWN TO GIVE WILLINGLY TO HIM

Paul and every Jew knew of occasions when God's people had given willingly. (See Exodus 35:4–36:7; 1 Chronicles 29:1-9.) Hundreds of years before Paul's time the people of God (Israelites) were in the wilderness traveling to the land God had promised them. On their way they needed a movable place of worship, a tabernacle. So God commanded the people to give willingly whatever they could for building the tabernacle. The richest gave gold and silver and precious jewels. Some women gave their metal mirrors. Others helped to spin and weave beautiful materials. Some men gave their time and skills to make the furnishings. Those who had nothing else to give searched for the wood needed for the altars, the table and the boards. That was a great gift because wood was scarce in the wilderness.

Show Illustration #13

All gave willingly. They gave what they could. They gave because they loved God. They gave so much that Moses finally had to tell them to stop giving. They had given more than enough!

2. GOD WANTS HIS OWN TO GIVE LIBERALLY

Not only are Christians to give willingly to God. They are to give liberally (with great generosity).

Show Illustration #14

Once when the Lord Jesus was at God's house in Jerusalem, He watched the people bringing their money. He saw the rich men giving large gifts. Then He saw a poor widow give two small coins worth less than a penny. The Lord Jesus said concerning her, "She has given more than all the rest. The others had plenty left after their gifts. But she gave all that she had."

A short time after the Lord Jesus went back to Heaven, there was a Jewish feast held in the city of Jerusalem. Many Jews had come for the occasion. While there, they heard the Gospel. Large numbers of them received the Lord Jesus Christ as Saviour. They stayed in the city to learn more about their new life. The Christians who lived in Jerusalem immediately shared whatever they could with these new believers.

Many were like Barnabas who sold his land and brought the money to the apostles. The apostles distributed the money to the poor so each one had what he/she needed. (See Acts 4:32-37.) The Christians were not required to do this. No one said, "You must sell your property and use your money in this way." But because of their love for the Lord, they gave liberally–some even giving all that they had.

3. GOD WANTS HIS OWN TO GIVE LOVINGLY

Not only are we to give willingly and liberally. We are to give lovingly.

Show Illustration #15

Once when Jesus was eating in the home of a Pharisee (a religious man who tried to keep the law), a woman who was a sinner brought an expensive jar of perfume to the house. She cried when she stood by the Lord Jesus and her tears wet His feet. She dried them with her hair and put the perfume on them. The Pharisee thought to himself: *If Jesus was really a prophet, He would know that this woman is a sinner.* Jesus knew what the man was thinking, so He said, "When I came into your house you didn't give Me water to wash My feet. [That was the usual custom in those days.] But she has washed My feet with her tears and dried them with her hair. You didn't kiss me. [This was how men greeted each other.] But she has kissed My feet ever since she came in. You didn't put oil on My head, but she has put perfume on My feet. She has done this because she loves much." To the woman He said, "Your sins are forgiven. Your faith has saved you from the penalty of sin." (See Luke 7:36-50.) She had given because she loved her Saviour.

Not many years ago in the land of Africa a great crowd of people gathered in a large church. The message about God's marvelous Gift, our Lord Jesus, had ended. A hush fell on all the people. Then suddenly one after another got up and brought a special gift for God. They wanted to thank Him for His dear Son who reconciled them to God. Some gave money; some gave their robes; and some gave bracelets and rings, head cloths and other things. All were piled on the platform.

One little boy in a tattered shirt and loin cloth sat watching with wide open eyes. Oh, if only he could bring something to the Saviour. Suddenly he jumped up, pulled off his shirt and went forward, placing his gift on the platform. He beamed as he stood there for a moment, as if giving not only the shirt, but himself as well. His face shone as he returned to his seat. He had given all he had. Do you think God was pleased?

If we truly love God, we will want to give Him whatever we can–even all that we can. Why do we love Him? Because He first loved us. (See 1 John 4:19.) God proved how much He loved us by sending His only Son into the world. The Lord Jesus proved His love for us by leaving the ivory palaces of Heaven (See Psalm 45:8.) and coming to this world to take the death punishment for our sins. (See 2 Corinthians 8:9; John 3:16; l John 3:16.) We prove our love for God and for His wonderful Gift by giving lovingly to Him. (See 2 Corinthians 9:15.)

4. CHRISTIANS ARE TO GIVE CHEERFULLY TO THE LORD

Show Illustration #16

Besides giving willingly and liberally and lovingly, we are taught to give cheerfully. (See 2 Corinthians 9:7.) If a farmer is stingy with his seed and plants only a little grain, he will have only a small harvest. A stingy farmer is miserable, you may be sure. He knows that for all his hard work he will have a poor crop. But a farmer who plants a lot of grain feels certain that he will have a big harvest, so he is cheerful. God says that cheerful giving is the kind that pleases Him. When we give to Him because we want to, He gives us everything we need. (See 2 Corinthians 9:8; Philippians 4:14-17, 19.)

Near the end of Paul's first letter to the Church at Corinth (16:2), we're told when we are to give, who is to give and how much we're to give. We must remember these three things:

1. The gifts we give to God are to be set aside on Sunday, the Lord's Day. (This first day of the week is the day of Christ's resurrection.) The Scriptures do not say much about what Christians should or should not do on the Lord's Day–Sunday. But besides worshiping the Lord, we are told to set aside our gifts for Him that day.
2. Gifts are to be given by each Christian, including children. It is a wonderful privilege to give to God. Because He made the world and all that is in it, He needs nothing from us. But He lets us–each one–give to Him.

3. Gifts are to be given in proportion to how God has given to us. For some this will mean giving large gifts. Others may be able to give only small gifts. But apparently God looks at what we have left after we give, rather than the amount we give. Everything we have is God's. We use just part of it for ourselves to keep us healthy and ready to serve God in all we do. (*Teacher:* please note: During Old Testament times God required the Jewish people to give a tenth of their income–called a tithe–to His servants, the Levites. See Numbers 18:21-30; Leviticus 27:30-33. In addition, a second tithe was to be set apart and eaten in a sacred meal in Jerusalem. See Deuteronomy 12:5-6, 11, 18. Every third year another tithe was taken for the Levites, the strangers, the fatherless and the widows. See Deuteronomy 14:28-29. But since New Testament times, Christians are to give as God has prospered them, remembering that everything belongs to Him. Certainly because of their love for the Saviour, Christians should give more than Jews were required to give.)

Because God gave, we give. We give because we want to give. We give because we love God and His Son who gave Himself for us–and we show that love in this way.

Giving to God is as important as any other service we do for Him. When we stand at the Judgment Seat of Christ, He will remember our gifts, as well as the other things we have done for Him. Are you faithful in your giving to Him? Have you given Him yourself? Would you like to do that right now?

REVIEW QUESTIONS

1. When Christians suffer in illness, in problems, in failure, in danger, or through death, to whom should they go first for help? *(To God. See memory verse, 1 Peter 5:7.)*
2. As we look at Paul's life for God, how can we tell that suffering doesn't always come because we have sinned? *(Paul, in his service for God, was constantly suffering because of His work, not because of sin.)*
3. When do you decide whether you will live in the future with God or be separated from Him forever? *(It must be before death, which may come at any time.)*
4. What part of a believer goes into the grave? *(The body only)*
5. Where will the believer's soul and spirit go when he or she dies? *(To be with God in a place of blessing)*
6. Who is an ambassador for Christ? *(God has made each believer a special representative and messenger of Christ.)*
7. What is the message of an ambassador of Christ? *(You must be reconciled to God.)*
8. How many believers have the responsibility to give the message of reconciliation? *(All believers)*
9. How are Christians to give to God? *(They are to give willingly, liberally, lovingly, cheerfully.)*
10. Why did Jesus say that the poor widow who gave two small coins gave more than all the rich men? *(The others had a lot left after their giving. She gave all she had.)*
11. Why did Jesus save the sinful woman from the penalty of sin? *(Because she trusted in Him)*
12. Why was Jesus pleased with the expensive gift the sinful woman had brought to Him? *(He knew that she trusted Him to save her from many sins and loved Him for it.)*
13. When are we to set aside our special gifts for God? *(On the first day of each week, the Lord's Day, the day specially set aside for worship)*
14. From whom does God want gifts? *(From every Christian, because in this way, we can share His wonderful work)*

www.ingramcontent.com/pod-product-compliance
Lightning Source LLC
Chambersburg PA
CBHW060802090426
42736CB00002B/124